EDGE BOOKS™

The Kids' Guide to
TITANIC

by Sean Stewart Price

Consultant:
Norm Lewis
President/Founder/CEO
Canadian Titanic Society (CTS)

CAPSTONE PRESS
a capstone imprint

Edge Books are published by Capstone Press,
1710 Roe Crest Drive, North Mankato, Minnesota 56003.
www.capstonepub.com

Books published by Capstone Press are manufactured with paper
containing at least 10 percent post-consumer waste.

Library of Congress Cataloging-in-Publication Data
Price, Sean.
  The kids' guide to Titanic / by Sean Stewart Price.
    p. cm.—(Edge books. Kids' guides.)
  Includes bibliographical references and index.
  Summary: "Discusses the Titanic, including its design, how the ship sank,
    the passengers on board, and why the ship's legacy lives on"—Provided
    by publisher.
  ISBN 978-1-4296-7661-8 (library binding)
  1. Titanic (Steamship)—Juvenile literature. 2. Shipwrecks—North Atlantic
    Ocean—Juvenile literature. I. Title. II. Series.
G530.T6P75 2012
910.9163'4—dc23   2011029262

Editorial Credits
Carrie Braulick Sheely, editor; Tracy Davies, designer; Wanda Winch, media
    researcher; Laura Manthe, production specialist

Photo Credits
Akg-images, 18, 21; Bridgeman Art Library: The Stapleton Collection
Private Collection, 22; Corbis: Bettmann, 5, Hulton-Deutsch Collection,
11, National Geographic Society, 1, 16, Ralph White, 15 (bottom);
Getty Images Inc: Dorling Kindersley, 20, National Geographic/Emory
Kristof, 26, 28-29; Library of Congress: Chronicling America Online
Collection, cover (top middle, right), Chronicling America Online
Collection/Library of Virginia, Richmond, VA, cover (top left), 19,
Prints and Photographs Division, 10, 14, 15 (top, middle); Mary Evans
Picture Library: Illustrated London News, 24, Onslow Auctions
Limited, 13; ©National Museums Northern Ireland, Collection Harland
& Wolff, Ulster Folk and Transport Museum, HOYFM.HW.H1726,
Titanic first class suite bedroom 'B60', March 1912, 12; Newscom:
Splash News and Pictures, 27; Painting by Ken Marschall, cover
©1982 (T1982c), 6 ©1992 (T1992d), 9 ©1997 (T1997e); Shutterstock:
AridOcean, 7 (bottom), Attsetski, scroll design, Flavia Morlachetti, 7
(postal design), WebStudio24h, back cover

:es of America in Stevens Point, Wisconsin.

12

Table of Contents

Chapter 1

BIRTH OF A LEGEND

Ettie Dean's husband, Bertram, woke her out of a sound sleep. He'd heard a giant crash. The Deans were **immigrants** from England bound for a new life in the United States. They were sailing on the RMS *Titanic*.

Bertram went to investigate and soon returned with terrible news. The ship had hit an iceberg. *Titanic* was sinking. Ettie bundled up her two children against the cold. The family then headed for *Titanic*'s lifeboats up on **deck**.

Titanic's deck was a mass of confusion. Most of the 2,208 passengers and crew were there. People were shouting and pushing to get on the lifeboats. Only 705 people made it. Ettie Dean and her two children were lucky. They found a place on a lifeboat. But her husband was never heard from again.

FACT: On May 31, 2009, Bertram and Ettie's daughter, Millvina, died at age 97. She had been the last living *Titanic* survivor.

Titanic's crew insisted that women and children board the lifeboats before the men.

immigrant—a person who leaves one country and settles in another

deck—the main floor of a boat or ship

Almost everything on *Titanic* had a touch of elegance, including its grand staircase. Only first-class passengers were allowed to use the staircase.

Bertran Dean was just one of 1,503 people to die when *Titanic* sank at 2:20 a.m. on April 15, 1912. The disaster shocked the world. *Titanic* was one of the largest and grandest ships ever to sail. People called it a floating palace. Some newspapers had declared the massive vehicle "unsinkable."

Titanic has fascinated people ever since it disappeared under the waves. If the great ship had missed the iceberg that Sunday, it would simply be remembered as a **luxurious** ocean liner. But so much went wrong that *Titanic* has become a symbol for disaster.

luxurious—made with expensive, beautiful features that provide comfort and pleasure, but that are not needed

What Does "RMS" Stand For?

RMS *Titanic* was a British ship. The ship carried mail as well as passengers. It took its name for the Royal Mail service that delivers mail in Britain. The initials "RMS" stand for Royal Mail Steamship. The ship is also sometimes called SS *Titanic.* The SS stands for "steamship."

TITANIC'S ROUTE

Atlantic Ocean

1. Belfast, Northern Ireland (sea trials)
2. Southampton, England (picks up first passengers)
3. Cherbourg, France
4. Queenstown, Ireland (picks up final passengers)
5. *Titanic* sinks
6. New York (planned final destination)

THE "UNSINKABLE" SHIP

For most of human history, crossing oceans has been very dangerous. But by the late 1800s, shipping companies were building giant metal steamships. These ships made sea crossings much safer.

Over time, shipping companies competed with one another to build bigger and better ships. This competition led the White Star Line to build *Titanic*. It was one of three similar, or "sister," ships. The other two ships were called *Olympic* and *Gigantic*. At the time, these three ships were the largest, most luxurious passenger ships ever built.

Titanic had many new safety features. One feature was its "watertight" compartments. The bottom of the ship was broken up into 16 compartments. A watertight wall called a bulkhead was between each compartment. The bulkheads extended well above the waterline. *Titanic* could float if any two of the compartments flooded, or even if the first four flooded. But if the first five flooded, the bow would begin sinking. The bulkheads were not completely sealed at the top. With the **bow** riding too low, water from the fifth compartment would overflow to the other compartments.

bow—the front end of a ship

bulkhead

©KEN MARSCHALL 1997

Many experts gave the compartment system excellent reviews. The British journal *The Shipbuilder* pronounced *Titanic* "practically unsinkable." Many people simply shortened that in their minds to "unsinkable."

FACTS ABOUT *TITANIC*

owner: White Star Line

builder: Harland and Wolff

length: 882.5 feet (269 meters)

width: 92.5 feet (28 meters)

weight: 46,328 tons (42,028 metric tons)

maximum number of passengers and crew: 3,500

number of passengers on board: 1,317

number of crew members on board: 891

top speed: about 28 miles (45 kilometers) per hour

number of lifeboats: 20

cost to build: $7.5 million in 1912 (about $164 million today)

* Some estimations of the cost to build the ship today are much higher, from $400 to $800 million.

A Shortage of Lifeboats

Titanic had lifeboat space for 1,176 people. At the time, British law required a ship of its size to have space for only 980 people. Legally, the ship had more than enough lifeboats. But *Titanic* still had far too few for the 2,208 passengers and crew on board.

Titanic's lifeboats

FACT: The name *Titanic* comes from the ancient Greek word "Titan." Titans were Greek gods known for their huge size and strength.

PASSENGER CLASSES

Like all luxury liners, *Titanic* divided passengers into classes. These three classes were based on ticket prices. A first-class ticket cost between $1,500 and $4,375 (about $33,000 to $95,000 today). At the time, a typical English home could be bought for about $1,000. First-class passengers had the fanciest rooms. They also were allowed to use a gym and swimming pool.

first-class room

A second-class ticket cost about $65 (about $1,400 today). These passengers had beautiful rooms as well. But they were not quite as nice as those in first class. Second-class passengers also had their own library and other pleasant places to enjoy the trip.

A third-class ticket cost about $36 (about $800 today). Third-class passengers had small, somewhat crowded rooms. These passengers also had little access to other parts of the ship. Still, third-class passengers on *Titanic* had much nicer living areas than passengers on other ships. Many third-class travelers were immigrants leaving Europe for a new life in the United States.

second-class room

THE RICH AND FAMOUS

The media called *Titanic* the "millionaire's special." Many rich and famous people were traveling on the new, luxurious ship. Their fortunes combined were roughly $500 million (about $11 billion today). These passengers included:

John Jacob and Madeleine Astor: This millionaire businessman and his wife were the richest people on board. Their fortune was worth nearly $2 billion in today's money. John died, but Madeleine survived.

John Jacob Astor

Madeleine Astor

Isidor and Ida Straus: Isidor was a businessman who helped start Macy's department store. Both Isidor and Ida died.

Archibald Butt: Archibald was a military advisor to U.S. President William Howard Taft. Archibald died when the ship sank.

Isidor Straus

Captain Edward Smith was known as the "millionaire's captain." He was given command of the White Star Line's most impressive ships. Many rich people liked to sail with him. Smith got along with them well and they enjoyed his company.

Smith ran a crew of nearly 900 people. Nine officers oversaw more than 300 stewards and stewardesses, who served the passengers' needs. These nine officers also oversaw the ship's mechanics and other workers.

Archibald Butt

Captain Edward Smith

FACT: People of at least 28 nationalities were among *Titanic*'s passengers and crew.

Chapter 2

DISASTER STRIKES

Titanic's crew had received several warnings of icebergs in the area before its crash.

"The passengers by this time were beginning to flock up on the boat deck, with anxious faces, the appalling din [noise from the escaping steam] only added to their anxiety in a situation already terrifying enough ... "

—Second Officer Charles Lightoller

"Iceberg! Right ahead!"

Those words rang out just before 11:40 on the night of April 14, 1912. They came from a person on *Titanic*'s **lookout**. The warning came too late. The great ship was already doomed. Within 40 seconds, the iceberg had ripped open the **starboard** side of the ship below the waterline.

People on *Titanic* felt the impact differently. Those closest to the iceberg were knocked off their feet. Bertram Dean and others who were farther away heard a loud crash or a ripping noise. Those farthest away felt only a small tremor and heard little or nothing.

After the ship hit the iceberg, an officer shut down the ship's engine. The built-up steam in the engines had to be released through escape valves. This process created a loud roar like several trains thundering by. The racket made it very difficult for anyone on the deck to be understood without shouting.

lookout—a high structure used for observation
starboard—the right side of a ship

Crew members struggled to keep order on the deck as they helped load the lifeboats.

SPREADING PANIC

Early on, many of *Titanic's* passengers hesitated to get into the lifeboats. They saw no need to leave the warm ship for a cold lifeboat. Most crew members did not realize how badly the iceberg had damaged the ship. Many encouraged passengers to relax. Twelve-year-old second-class passenger Ruth Becker heard one crew member explain that the compartments would keep the ship afloat until help arrived.

But an hour and a half after the collision, many people realized that the ship was sinking. By then, the terrible noise from the steam had finally stopped. The shouting and clamor of thousands of people on deck could then be heard. The ship's small orchestra began playing popular tunes to help keep people calm.

At about the same time, *Titanic*'s crew began firing distress rockets in the air. These exploding rockets looked like fireworks. They were designed to get the attention of other ships. Anyone who doubted *Titanic*'s distress before now understood that everyone on board was in terrible danger.

The effort to load and launch the lifeboats became increasingly frantic. A survivor remembered watching an officer load people. " … [He] was getting the children and chucking them into the boat. Mr. Murdoch [an officer] and the baker [the officer loading] made the women jump across into the boat about two feet and a half … He threw them [the children] onto the women and he was catching children by their dresses and chucking them in … "

TITANIC SANK IN STAGES:

1. Water filled up the watertight compartments in the bow.

2. As the bow filled with water, the **stern** rose out of the water.

3. The weight of the water in the bow caused the ship to become nearly vertical. This position put stress on the hull.

4. Eventually, the ship broke into two main sections. The bow sank.

5. The stern righted itself briefly. But water flooded in. The stern soon joined the bow on the ocean's bottom.

As *Titanic* sank, almost all of the passengers left aboard wound up in the frigid Atlantic Ocean. The water temperature was about 28 degrees Fahrenheit (minus 2 degrees Celsius). A temperature that low can kill people within minutes by causing **hypothermia**.

One survivor described the agony of hitting the water. "I hung on by the rail [of the sinking ship] and then let myself drop into the sea. The distance to the water was 75 feet, and I thought I was never going to get there. When I did come into contact with the water, it was like a great knife cutting into me. My limbs and body ached for days afterward."

Most of the people in the water wore life jackets. But victims were helpless against the cold temperatures.

stern—the back part of a ship

hypothermia—a life-threatening condition that occurs when a person's body temperature falls several degrees below normal

Chapter 3

TERRIBLE AFTERMATH

People in *Titanic*'s lifeboats rowed aimlessly in the ocean for hours.

At 2:20 a.m., *Titanic*'s 20 lifeboats were all that remained of the great ship above water. They held just more than 700 freezing passengers. Many hoped that loved ones had somehow made it onto other lifeboats. None of them knew if a rescue ship would arrive.

Right after *Titanic* sank, the people in the water shouted for help from those in the lifeboats. Survivors said the roar sounded like a ballpark crowd cheering a home run.

Despite the loud cries, only lifeboat No. 14 went back to pick up people in the water. People in the other lifeboats were afraid to do so. They feared their lifeboats would be pulled down by the suction from the sinking *Titanic*. However, there was barely any suction as the ship sank. People in the lifeboats were also afraid of their boats being overturned or overwhelmed by people scrambling aboard.

WHAT WAS LEARNED

At 4:10 a.m., not quite two hours after *Titanic* sank, a rescue ship began picking up survivors. Captain Arthur Rostron had raced *Carpathia* to the scene. It ran an obstacle course of icebergs to get there. Within a few hours, *Carpathia* sailed off to New York with 705 *Titanic* survivors.

photograph of *Titanic* survivors on *Carpathia*

There were two investigations into *Titanic*'s sinking. One was American and one was British. The investigations soon changed the way ships operated:

- New laws stated that all ships had to have enough lifeboats for everyone on board.

- All shipping lanes were shifted farther south to avoid icebergs.

- An iceberg patrol was set up. Ships in the patrol roamed the North Atlantic and warned other ships about icebergs in the area.

Another change involved the use of wireless radios. As *Titanic* sank, some passengers and crew saw the lights of a ship in the distance. But that ship did nothing to save people on *Titanic*.

Californian was accused of being the mystery ship. Later investigations found that this may not have been true. A third ship may have moved between them. Even so, *Californian* was close enough to save people on *Titanic*. But it never heard the distress message because its radio was shut off for the night. This practice was common at the time. It ended after *Titanic*'s sinking.

Chapter 4

TITANIC'S LEGACY

Titanic's bow at the bottom
of the Atlantic Ocean

FACT: Thousands of objects have been taken from *Titanic's* resting place and brought to museums. These items include everything from children's marbles to ship parts. But many people think that the shipwreck should be left alone.

In 1985 Frenchman Jean-Louis Michel and American Robert Ballard led the team of scientists that discovered *Titanic*'s wreck. The great ship's remains had sunk nearly 2.5 miles (4 kilometers) below the Atlantic Ocean's surface. The discovery ended decades of guesswork. People finally knew exactly where *Titanic* sank. They also found out that the ship had broken in two. Before its discovery, people disagreed on whether the ship had stayed in one piece.

As soon as *Titanic* sank, people wondered if a design flaw might have helped cause its sinking. Some experts thought the **rivets** were to blame. Discovery of the wreck showed that this rumor was true. The metal in *Titanic*'s rivets contained impurities that made them weak. As a result, the rivets' heads popped off when the ship scraped the iceberg. The metal plates then separated, letting in water.

Titanic's hull rivets

rivet—a headed metal pin or bolt used for joining two pieces of a material together

TITANIC TIMELINE

1912

April 10
Titanic makes its first official voyage with passengers from Southampton, England, to Cherbourg, France.

April 13
Titanic gets the first of seven warnings about icebergs in the North Atlantic from other ships.

April 15, 12:00 a.m.
Captain Smith orders the ship's wireless operators to send a distress call.

12:05 a.m.
Smith orders the crew to get the lifeboats ready to use.

April 10–11
Titanic leaves Cherbourg on April 10. It arrives at Queenstown (now Cobh), Ireland, on April 11 to pick up its final passengers. The ship leaves for New York.

April 14
Around 11:40 p.m., *Titanic* collides with an iceberg while traveling at almost 25 miles (40 km) per hour. Within 10 minutes, Captain Smith and ship designer Thomas Andrews check for damage. Andrews tells the captain that the ship will sink in about two hours.

12:25 a.m.
Smith orders passengers into the lifeboats, women and children first.

Titanic's sinking has inspired many books, plays, movies, and songs. The first movie came out just one month after the ship sank. It starred survivor Dorothy Gibson. She wore the dress she had been rescued in.

12:30 a.m.
Passengers remain hesitant to board the lifeboats. Most people on board do not yet realize the seriousness of the damage to the ship.

12:45 a.m.
Lifeboat No. 7 is the first lowered into the water. *Titanic* fires the first of eight distress rockets into the air. The sight of the rockets convinces passengers that the ship is really in trouble.

2:05 a.m.
The last lifeboat is launched. More than 1,500 people remain on the ship.

2:17 a.m.
Titanic's last wireless message is sent. Captain Smith tells several crew members, "It's every man for himself."

2:18 a.m.
Titanic breaks in two pieces. The bow section sinks. The stern section stays afloat.

2:20 a.m.
The last of *Titanic* disappears beneath the waves.

3:30 a.m.
The survivors in the lifeboats see signal rockets from *Carpathia*, a ship coming to the rescue.

4:10 a.m.
Lifeboat No. 2 is the first boat picked up by *Carpathia*.

8:30 a.m.
Survivors in lifeboat No. 12 are the last rescued. Three days later, *Carpathia* arrives in New York with 705 *Titanic* survivors.

Today *Titanic* exhibits can be found throughout the world at museums. Thousands of people visit the exhibits each year. They show that interest in *Titanic*'s story will go on.

Glossary

bow (BAU)—the front end of a ship

bulkhead (BULK-hed)—an upright wall separating compartments

deck (DEK)—the main floor of a boat or ship

hull (HUL)—the main body of a boat or ship

hypothermia (hye-puh-THUR-mee-uh)—a life-threatening condition that occurs when a person's body temperature falls several degrees below normal

immigrant (IM-uh-gruhnt)—a person who leaves one country and settles in another

lookout (LUK-owt)—a high structure used for observation

luxurious (LUHG-zhur-ee-uhs)—made with expensive, beautiful features that provide comfort and pleasure, but that are not needed

rivet (RI-vuht)—a headed metal pin or bolt used for joining two pieces of a material together

starboard (STAR-burd)—the right side of a ship

stern (STERN)—the back end of a ship

Read More

Adams, Simon. *Titanic*. DK Eyewitness Books. New York: DK Pub., 2009.

Biskup, Agnieszka. *Exploring Titanic: An Isabel Soto History Adventure.* Graphic Expeditions. Mankato, Minn.: Capstone Press, 2010.

Burgan, Michael. *Titanic: Truth and Rumors.* Truth and Rumors. Mankato, Minn.: Capstone Press, 2010.

Brown, Don. *All Stations! Distress!: April 15, 1912, the Day the Titanic Sank.* New York: Flash Point/ Roaring Book Press, 2008.

Internet Sites

FactHound offers a safe, fun way to find Internet sites related to this book. All of the sites on FactHound have been researched by our staff.

Here's all you do:

Visit *www.facthound.com*

Type in this code: 9781429676618

 **Super-cool stuff!** Check out projects, games and lots more at
www.capstonekids.com

Index